Your Government:
How It Works

How to Become
an Elected Official

Mike Bonner

Arthur M. Schlesinger, jr.
Senior Consulting Editor

Chelsea House Publishers
Philadelphia

This book is dedicated to the memory of my father, James Joseph Bonner, 1922–1968, who always wanted to run for office but never got the chance.

CHELSEA HOUSE PUBLISHERS
Editor in Chief Stephen Reginald
Production Manager Pamela Loos
Art Director Sara Davis
Director of Photography Judy L. Hasday
Managing Editor James D. Gallagher
Senior Production Editor LeeAnne Gelletly

Staff for HOW TO BECOME AN ELECTED OFFICIAL
Project Editor Anne Hill
Project Editor/Publishing Coordinator Jim McAvoy
Associate Art Director Takeshi Takahashi
Series Designer Takeshi Takahashi, Keith Trego

The Chelsea House World Wide Web address is
http://www.chelseahouse.com

3 5 7 9 8 6 4 2

Library of Congress Cataloging-in-Publication Data

Bonner, Mike, 1951–
    How to become an elected official / by Mike Bonner.
        p. cm. — (Your government—how it works)
    Includes bibliographical references and index.
    Summary: Explains the process of running and campaigning for public office, covering such topics as the decision to run, making contacts, and fundraising.
    ISBN 0-7910-5536-1 (hc)
    1. Electioneering—United States—Juvenile literature. 2. Campaign management—United States—Juvenile literature. 3. Public officers—United States—Juvenile literature [1. Elections. 2. Politics, Practical.] I. Title. II. Series.

JK2281 .B66 2000
324.7'0973—dc21   99-048461

Contents

Government:
Crises of Confidence
Arthur M. Schlesinger, jr.   5

1 **Deciding to Run**   9

2 **Making Contacts**   17

3 **Following the Money**   25

4 **Campaigning to Win**   35

5 **Fighting Back Effectively**   45

6 **Making a Difference**   53

Glossary   60

Further Reading   62

Index   63

YOUR GOVERNMENT
HOW IT WORKS

The Central Intelligence Agency

The Federal Bureau of Investigation

The History of the Democratic Party

The History of the Republican Party

The History of Third Parties

The House of Representatives

How a Bill Is Passed

How to Become an Elected Official

The Impeachment Process

The Presidency

The Senate

The Supreme Court

Introduction

Government: Crises of Confidence

Arthur M. Schlesinger, jr.

FROM THE START, Americans have regarded their government with a mixture of reliance and mistrust. The men who founded the republic understood the importance of government. "If men were angels," observed the 51st Federalist Paper, "no government would be necessary." But men are not angels. Because human beings are subject to wicked as well as to noble impulses, government was deemed essential to assure freedom and order.

The American revolutionaries, however, also knew that government could become a source of injury and oppression. The men who gathered in Philadelphia in 1787 to write the Constitution therefore had two purposes in mind: They wanted to establish a strong central authority and to limit that central authority's capacity to abuse its power.

To prevent the abuse of power, the Founding Fathers wrote two basic principles into the Constitution. The principle of federalism divided power between the state governments and the central authority. The principle of the separation of powers subdivided the central authority itself into three branches—the executive, the legislative, and the judiciary—so that "each may be a check on the other."

YOUR GOVERNMENT: HOW IT WORKS examines some of the major parts of that central authority, the federal government. It explains how various officials, agencies, and departments operate and explores the political organizations that have grown up to serve the needs of government.

Introduction

The federal government as presented in the Constitution was more an idealistic construct than a practical administrative structure. It was barely functional when it came into being.

This was especially true of the executive branch. The Constitution did not describe the executive branch in any detail. After vesting executive power in the president, it assumed the existence of "executive departments" without specifying what these departments should be. Congress began defining their functions in 1789 by creating the Departments of State, Treasury, and War.

President Washington, assisted by Secretary of the Treasury Alexander Hamilton, equipped the infant republic with a working administrative structure. Congress also continued that process by creating more executive departments as they were needed.

Throughout the 19th century, the number of federal government workers increased at a consistently faster rate than did the population. Increasing concerns about the politicization of public service led to efforts—bitterly opposed by politicians—to reform it in the latter part of the century.

The 20th century saw considerable expansion of the federal establishment. More importantly, it saw growing impatience with bureaucracy in society as a whole.

The Great Depression during the 1930s confronted the nation with its greatest crisis since the Civil War. Under Franklin Roosevelt, the New Deal reshaped the federal government, assigning it a variety of new responsibilities and greatly expanding its regulatory functions. By 1940, the number of federal workers passed the 1 million mark.

Critics complained of big government and bureaucracy. Business owners resented federal regulation. Conservatives worried about the impact of paternalistic government on self-reliance, on community responsibility, and on economic and personal freedom.

When the United States entered World War II in 1941, government agencies focused their energies on supporting the war effort. By the end of World War II, federal civilian employment had risen to 3.8 million. With peace, the federal establishment declined to around 2 million in 1950. Then growth resumed, reaching 2.8 million by the 1980s.

A large part of this growth was the result of the national government assuming new functions such as: affirmative action in civil rights, environmental protection, and safety and health in the workplace.

Some critics became convinced that the national government was a steadily growing behemoth swallowing up the liberties of the people. The 1980s brought new intensity to the debate about government growth. Foes of Washington bureaucrats preferred local government, feeling it more responsive to popular needs.

But local government is characteristically the government of the locally powerful. Historically, the locally powerless have often won their human and constitutional rights by appealing to the national government. The national government has defended racial justice against local bigotry, upheld the Bill of Rights against local vigilantism, and protected natural resources from local greed. It has civilized industry and secured the rights of labor organizations. Had the states' rights creed prevailed, perhaps slavery would still exist in the United States.

Americans are still of two minds. When pollsters ask large, spacious questions—Do you think government has become too involved in your lives? Do you think government should stop regulating business?—a sizable majority opposes big government. But when asked specific questions about the practical work of government—Do you favor Social Security? Unemployment compensation? Medicare? Health and safety standards in factories? Environmental protection?—a sizable majority approves of intervention.

We do not like bureaucracy, but we cannot live without it. We need its genius for organizing the intricate details of our daily lives. Without bureaucracy, modern society would collapse. It would be impossible to run any of the large public and private organizations we depend on without bureaucracy's division of labor and hierarchy of authority. The challenge is to keep these necessary structures of our civilization flexible, efficient, and capable of innovation.

More than 200 years after the drafting of the Constitution, Americans still rely on government but also mistrust it. These attitudes continue to serve us well. What we mistrust, we are more likely to monitor. And government needs our constant attention if it is to avoid inefficiency, incompetence, and arbitrariness. Without our informed participation, it cannot serve us individually or help us as a people to attain the lofty goals of the Founding Fathers.

New Jersey Governor Christine Todd Whitman celebrates her victory with supporters on election night 1997. The decision to run is the only decision an elected official must make on his or her own.

CHAPTER

1

Deciding to Run

Losers Are Still Winners

ON ELECTION NIGHT THE tension rises as votes are counted. Television broadcasters around the nation review each race for Congress, the state legislatures, and thousands of local, city, and county contests. As voters leave the polling places, some candidates are winners and others are losers. Only the narrowest races still hang in the balance by midnight. Come morning, nearly all the close races will tally final results. The long, difficult election process has ended.

At **campaign** headquarters, the friends and family of the winners cheer and congratulate the victor. Elsewhere, the losers hear condolences and sympathetic words. In the mind and heart of every candidate, winner or loser, there is pride, satisfaction, and occasionally, regret.

Elections are a big business in the United States. Every even-numbered year elections are held to select the people who will occupy public offices. Special elections are occasionally needed to fill vacancies resulting from the death or resignation of an officeholder.

Large and small cities conduct "off year" elections to choose new mayors and city council members.

Every four years an election is held to decide who will be the president. Members of the House of Representatives are elected every two years. Senators serve six-year terms, with one-third of that body being up for election every two years.

Most of the important decisions in the United States are made by elected officials. They determine what policies local, state, and the national government must follow. Becoming an elected official is one of the toughest tasks a person can undertake.

Becoming an elected official, however, can be highly rewarding. When you are an elected official, you have a large say in the operation of a sprawling government enterprise. You can raise or lower taxes. You can say who gets health care and who does not. You make the decision if a natural environment gets paved over to make way for new roads, businesses, and housing developments. If you think it is good policy to do so, you can preserve that same environment.

You, the elected official, are in charge of making policy. People look to you for answers because you have the power.

Despite your status as an official, however, you never act alone. Many other people help you decide policy at every stage of the process. For example, you have your family, your friends, your advisers, the voters, the lobbyists, your staff, the public, and your fellow officials to help you make the decisions.

The one decision you must make on your own, however, is the decision to compete for elective office. No one else can make it for you. There is drama and danger in making the decision. Former President Nixon found running for office so exciting and challenging that he called it "The Arena."

Running for office involves weighing the risks of the race against the possible benefits. A common misconception about the pursuit of elective office is that the loser is somehow badly affected afterwards. This is often not true. Political scientists who study campaigns now say that even losing an election has a hidden positive side. There are social and financial benefits in trying to become an elected official.

For example, if a candidate wants to run again, for the same office or another one, the loser enjoys an enhanced position by gaining name familiarity. If the candidate happens to be in a business where being known in the community is a help, like real estate, law, or sales, name familiarity is a solid asset that brings in customers.

Even though a candidate loses an election, he or she may still regard the campaign as a success. A close election run against the incumbent candidate can build the reputation of the loser. Voters will remember the candidate and his or her message—especially if they become angry at something the incumbent does while in office. After the election, the losing candidate may remain in the public eye by speaking out against the incumbent's policies. The increased name recognition that results may help the candidate in the next election.

Not everyone has the stomach to run for public office. Politics is a rough and tumble game. It takes a special sort of person to be able to read negative or embarrassing things about himself or herself in the local newspaper and not get too upset.

You also have to be fairly strong-minded to have someone speak against you on television or the radio and not get angry, at least not in public. People who run for elective office encounter many insulting words and deeds, often from strangers who know them only by reputation.

Even the highest elected officeholders are regularly subjected to the most humiliating scrutiny. It's all a part of the job. To be successful, candidates have to put the bad parts behind them as quickly as possible and keep on running.

Types of Candidates

Many types of candidates seek elected office. The most common type is the recruited candidate. A recruited

Democratic presidential candidate Governor Michael Dukakis of Massachusetts faced unwelcome publicity when his wife, Kitty (left), publicly admitted that she had sought treatment for a drinking problem.

candidate is someone other people believe would make a good elected official. Large companies that are heavily regulated by government agencies often encourage their employees to become elected officials.

Such companies are found in the transportation, utility, medical, banking, legal, and insurance industries, to name a few. These interests depend on friends in public office to help them maintain a strong position in their business fields.

Recruited candidates also come from the political parties. Elections that feature opposing party candidates are called *partisan races.* Although the influence of political parties has greatly diminished from what it was in years past, the parties are still a major factor in elections. Parties try to recruit candidates for partisan races because without a candidate, the party would have no chance of winning the office. Holding public offices is vital to political parties.

The good thing about being a recruited candidate is the base of support you can count on from your sponsors. They can provide you with money, advice, and volunteers, which makes winning much easier than going into a race without sponsors. The bad thing about being a recruited candidate is that your sponsors expect you to support their point of view. This may limit your freedom of action and eventually turn you into little more than an agent of the group that sponsored you.

Most of the people who eventually wind up in elected office are recruited candidates. They are usually middle-aged people who have established solid reputations in their communities. They run businesses, teach school, control unions, practice law, or do any of a hundred different things that make them prominent in their communities. In many cases they are the natural leaders of the places where they live.

Once they get elected, they are the official leaders of their communities as well. So if they act as agents of their sponsoring groups, they are usually willing agents.

Another type of candidate is the self-starter. Abraham Lincoln is a good example of the self-starting candidate. He grew up with a strong interest in politics and public affairs. Once he was old enough to become a candidate, Lincoln ran for his first elective office. He lost.

Undeterred, Lincoln ran again and won. In the course of his political career, Lincoln lost many races. He even lost a senate race to Stephen Douglas in 1858, for a seat he had his heart set on winning. During the race Lincoln debated Douglas in a string of famous appearances throughout Illinois. Following his defeat by Douglas, Lincoln coined an oft-quoted statement about losing an election:

"I feel like the boy who stumped his toe," Lincoln said. "I am too big to cry and too badly hurt to laugh."

Two years later, Lincoln came back to win the presidency, beating Douglas and two other candidates.

Most self-starting candidates are people who, like Lincoln, show a strong interest in politics at an early age. They usually make every effort to advance themselves and their careers. In school they run for class offices. They are outgoing and like to be around people. They have many friends but they may also have some enemies, frequently other self-starters.

Elected officials at the highest level are typically self-starters. A nickname for self-starters is "whirlybirds," because they take off by themselves. One quality that such candidates share is ambition. Scratch the surface of a

Two years after Abraham Lincoln debated Stephen Douglas (right) for a seat in the Illinois senate and lost, he defeated Douglas in the 1860 presidential elections.

self-starter and you will probably find a young man or a young woman who wants to be president someday.

No matter what their background or beliefs, most candidates are idealistic. Lots of youthful idealists enter politics but they burn out quickly once they find out how grueling it is to seek office. They have good intentions but lack the necessary drive to make their dream of holding office come true.

Representative Floyd Prozanski, a state legislator from Oregon, is an example of one who made it happen. Prozanski said he had the best intentions when he decided to seek office. "I wanted to represent my district and develop sound statewide public policies to ensure the quality of life for all Oregonians," Prozanski said.

Elected officials can do enormous good if they are tough and operate on behalf of sound principles. They can get laws passed that improve schools, promote justice, help the poor, save money, and protect the natural environment.

President John F. Kennedy (seated) signs three new bills to create tough anti-crime laws in 1961. Attorney General Robert Kennedy (directly behind the president) was known for his vigorous prosecution of civil rights cases.

They can also stop bad laws and block poorly thought out schemes by other officials. The best elected officials will fight corruption, support reform, and persuade people to act and think in a more responsible fashion. These opportunities are a powerful draw for people who see things that trouble them in society.

Before his death in 1968, Senator Robert F. Kennedy often quoted the French philosopher Albert Camus to express why he was involved in public life and the pursuit of elective office. "Perhaps we cannot prevent this from being a world in which children are tortured," Kennedy said. "But we can reduce the number of tortured children."

Once you have made the decision to run for office, you must, as a candidate, turn your attention to the knotty mechanics of the election process. A huge variety of complicated issues must be addressed if you are going to run a good race. To give yourself a decent chance at success, you must start making contacts.

First Lady Hillary Clinton, shown speaking at a June 1999 fundraiser, used an exploratory committee to rate her chances of being elected as a senator for New York state.

Making Contacts

IN MOST SOCIETIES, POLITICS is a war waged by the wealthy against the other social classes. Politics in the United States is not much different. But rather than use weapons and armies, Americans fight their political battles with elections, ballots, rallies, slogans, and **advertising** campaigns.

Fortunately for us, Americans have a long and precious tradition of accepting whoever gets elected to office. The founders of our republic believed life would be a lot better if there were some reliable nonviolent way for us to hash out our differences. This is the reason we have elections. Candidates are the front-line soldiers of the American political process. They take the shots when opposing groups dispute the policies of our government.

Our election system has broken down only once. In 1860, 11 Southern states refused to accept the election of Abraham Lincoln as president. They left the Union and bombarded federal property at Fort

Sumter a few months later. After four years of fierce fighting, the Northern states won the Civil War. By doing so, the idea that a U.S. election could be nullified by armed force was permanently discredited.

Primaries and General Elections

There are two main kinds of elections, primaries and **general elections.** A **primary election** precedes a general election. A primary narrows the field down to a couple of candidates, who then face each other in a general election. To borrow a concept from sports, a primary election is like a quarterfinal or a semifinal game.

A general election is the finals of politics. In some elections, if a candidate wins the primary by more than 50 percent of the vote, he or she gets to appear on the general election ballot all by himself or herself.

Filing for elective office is required before a candidate may formally seek the job. Filing usually requires the payment of a fee and guarantees that the candidate's name will appear on the primary election ballot.

The filing officer for city and county offices is usually the recorder or auditor for that jurisdiction. Most counties employ a special officer to oversee elections. State elections officers are commonly known as secretaries of state. These state officers often have duties besides elections, but not always.

Once you have filed as a candidate, the public knows you are planning to run for office.

However, nothing prevents you from making exploratory contacts before filing. Campaign manuals frequently recommend that you delay filing until a favorable moment. During the summer of 1999, for example, First Lady Hillary Clinton formed an exploratory committee to look into her chances of winning a U.S Senate seat in New York. Such preliminary contacts are useful in determining whether a person has enough potential support to make a reasonable run at the job.

Not everyone runs for office with the express goal of becoming an elected official. Some run without any expectation of victory. They want to raise interest in an issue, make a point, support their party, or simply get attention. Some run just to settle an old score with an opponent. Reasons for running are as varied as individual human beings. For a serious candidate, however, the goal is victory. Making the right contacts in a timely manner can spell the difference between victory or defeat.

Power Brokers

Most government decisions are supposed to be made out in the open in a democracy. Some decisions take place behind closed doors, but they are supposed to be the exceptions. Unfortunately, many truly important decisions are made in a secretive manner. The people who make these important decisions go by a variety of names. Here we will call them "power brokers."

Seeking to become an elected official enrolls you in the same club as the power brokers. When you become a candidate for elective office, the power brokers definitely want to know who you are and what you are about. They do this because they are intensely interested in seeing who gets elected to public office.

The first stop for any serious candidate is with the power brokers who influence elections. In a local race like a city election, the power brokers are generally the same people who do business with the city. They include current elected officials, planners, land developers, business owners, investors, and real estate professionals. Other influential people are neighborhood leaders, union representatives, citizen activists, and top-appointed officials of the city government.

For statewide and national offices, the main power brokers are of a similar type. The chief difference is that they cover a much broader territory.

Knowing how to approach the power brokers is critically important to your success. Approaching an important source of support is like any job interview. You will want to put aside your own issues and tell the power brokers why supporting you will benefit them. The best strategy is to be well-prepared, relaxed, and confident.

Before making contact, the candidate should try to learn as much as possible about potential supporters. This means finding out about them personally as well as finding out about their views on issues. It is crucial to stay informed about your potential supporters or you'll risk making a mistake.

You should act as if you know their problems almost as well as they do without sounding condescending. You

James McDougal, one of President Bill Clinton's partners in the Whitewater real estate investment deal, was later jailed on fraud and conspiracy charges.

should be sympathetic and realistic, but you should avoid making any promises other than the promise to listen and be fair. At the conclusion of the interview, you should make a strong pitch for an endorsement.

As a candidate you will be confronted, over and over again, with interest groups that are opposed to each other. Of course you would like to have the support of both sides. They will not often go for that, however, unless you have a very weak opponent or no opponent at all. Whatever you do, don't offer to support any side without knowing what both sides are asking.

Door-to-Door Campaigning

While you are courting the power brokers, many campaign manuals recommend going out among the people to find out what they are thinking. In small districts, like a state legislative or city council seat, an excellent way of making contacts is going door-to-door.

A candidate should take along a handy brochure or a flyer (it doesn't have to be much) and a batch of voter registration cards. Your name should be in big letters on all your material. Knocking on every door and introducing yourself is a good way to see how people react to you.

In most places a typical district will contain a large number of middle-income areas, some low-income areas, and a few high-income areas. If you have a good personality and are well-spoken, you can win a lot of votes going door-to-door.

A candidate who is unafraid to go out among the people will also impress the power brokers. Low-visibility races, like the ones for state legislative seats, city council seats, and county commission seats, are tempting targets for an aggressive street campaign. The power brokers know this as well.

A typical greeting is to give your name and the office you are running for. Ask if you may leave one of your brochures behind. Make sure they are registered voters. If not, ask them to complete a voter registration card on the spot.

Going door-to-door can provide the candidate with a wealth of information about the people. You learn who is home during the day and who is not. You find out many things about the people in your district. You may learn to your surprise how many of your neighbors dislike each other. As a candidate for public office, people will describe their hopes and dreams to you. It is at once fascinating and deeply moving.

You will learn who has well-cared-for children and who has neglected or abused children. In the poorer neighborhoods, you will see and hear much that disturbs you. You may wake up in the night, thinking about a particular face or about something that was said to you.

There will be many touching moments. Sometimes people will hear your pitch and announce that they are going to support you.

"We need to elect somebody like you," they will say. You may be carrying not only your own hopes but the hopes of hundreds or possibly thousands of others on your shoulders.

Much of what you learn probably will not be a surprise. The people who are poor will voice their suspicion that wealthy and powerful individuals manipulate the system to their advantage. They will complain that most, if not all, politicians are "bought and paid for." Then they may judge you and your candidacy.

In the more affluent neighborhoods people may brag about their political connections. Some ask pointed questions to see if you are willing to support their privileges. You'd better have a good answer ready or they will be quick to slam the door.

Walking the streets while talking to the power brokers at the same time is a superb political education. At some

point all your plans and schemes will take second place to simply going out among the people. You explain what you are doing and listen to what they have to say. The collective wisdom of the people will give you a true picture of the challenges you face in your quest to become an elected official.

Republican presidential candidate Pat Buchanan (left) and his campaign manager (right) telephone New Hampshire voters in 1996.

Elizabeth Dole, shown with her husband, former senator Bob Dole, dropped out of the race for the 2000 Republican presidential nomination because she said rival candidates Steve Forbes and Governor George W. Bush enjoyed a significant economical advantage.

CHAPTER 3

Following the Money

Campaign Costs

RUNNING FOR ALMOST ANY public office is expensive. Politics has always been an expensive enterprise. The humorist Will Rogers said back in 1931 that "politics has got so expensive that it takes lots of money to even get beat with."

Rogers's joke never grows old. Campaign costs rise as the stakes rise. During the 1998 election, candidates for seats in the U.S. House of Representatives spent $387 million on 435 races. The individual Senate races run in 1998 cost substantially more each. Spending on 33 seats topped $243 million. A few years earlier one California congressman spent $30 million from his wealthy family's fortune in the hopes of winning a seat in the U.S. Senate. However, he lost anyway.

State legislative seats are also growing ever more expensive. The political watchdog group Common Cause has figures showing that an entry-level state representative job can cost upwards of $250,000. Most of the money in the big races gets spent on slick television advertising. In the smaller races candidates spend money on printing, buttons, bumper stickers, direct mailing of brochures, radio ads, yard signs, and billboards.

Nothing comes cheap. Basic printed brochures and flyers cost about five cents each in lots of ten and twenty thousand. The more elaborate they are, the more they cost. Yard signs made from recycled plastic cost about three to four dollars each, not counting artwork, set-up, wooden stakes, and hardware.

Bumper stickers cost at least 50 cents each to produce. Buttons and labels are about the same. Remember that everything has to be produced in huge lots. Every congressional district contains just under half a million people. Council, commission, and legislative districts might be smaller in size, but they are just as expensive per voter.

The items mentioned here are just the most obvious campaign tools. Not included are special polls, make-over sessions, speech coaches, researchers, and radio and television specialists. These can add thousands to your budget.

Republican presidential candidate Lamar Alexander visits workers at his headquarters in Des Moines, Iowa, in 1999. Maintaining campaign headquarters is a major expense in a national campaign.

Sources of Campaign Money

Where does all the money come from? A basic fact of life in our political system is that campaign money comes from people who want things from the government. It is unrealistic to pretend otherwise. Organizations who have ideas to sell will spend money, often big money, to elect their friends.

Most of the money is funneled through groups called **political action committees,** or PACs. These committees collect money from their members and friends. The PAC then donates the group's money to favored political candidates. These donations are called campaign contributions. Political candidates use campaign contributions to finance their elections.

Accepting a campaign contribution usually means that the politician must give the donor group special consideration. This is mostly done by unspoken agreement. In the halls of government, the special consideration given to campaign donors goes by the code name "courtesy."

Former U.S. Senator Bob Dole, the 1996 Republican candidate for president, once told the honest truth about PACs. "When special interests contribute money, they want something in return other than good government," Dole said.

At present, campaign money and free speech are considered the same thing. Consequently, there are few limits on it. The key ruling in this regard was a 1976 U.S. Supreme Court decision, *Buckley v. Vallejo.* The court established political money as a form of free speech and held that restrictive limits on it were therefore unconstitutional.

The people with the most free speech instantly became the people with the most money. Federal Elections Commission reports show that the biggest contributors are commercial **corporations.** The American political scene is dominated by such corporations. Some political scientists have described this domination as a **hegemony.** That means they are the chief influence in our society. Corporations are active in the state legislatures and everywhere else

Consumer activist Ralph Nader, shown testifying before a consumer affairs committee in Washington, D.C., represents the anticorporate view of American culture.

where decisions are made that affect business. The managers of the corporations say their efforts are necessary to preserve a healthy economy and ensure progress.

Anticorporate activists complain that corporate interests are so dominant that the culture of commerce leads us away from our best human qualities. Vocal critics like consumer activist Ralph Nader say that the commercial culture turns us into product consumers, not people. We are at the point, they say, where our status is determined by how big our houses are and how many possessions we have. The content of our character, our goodness, and our zest for living is made to seem less important than taking expensive vacations and buying all the latest toys, clothes, and gadgets.

As an overriding concern, they say, the pollution we generate from our heated economic activity poisons the Earth and deprives Third World countries of a decent standard of living.

Opposing views of American commercial culture are at the heart of most conflicts in our political system. Anyone who wants to become an elected official must somehow grapple with these opposing views. A few candidates try to solve the problem by swinging back and forth between the two sides. Most others stand by the commercial corporations much of the time.

The PACs are the spearheads of the commercial culture. The richest PACs are vehicles of the big national and multinational corporations. They raise vast sums of money from employees and stockholders for political purposes.

Corporations aren't the only PAC players. Trade unions, special-interest groups, and private organizations also operate PACs. The unions raise and spend about $40 million every two years on political campaigns.

Private issue groups, like the Conservative PAC, the Sierra Club, and the Right to Life PAC raise and spend about $20 million every two years on political campaigns.

Hard Money, Soft Money, and PACs

Special laws govern the raising and spending of political money. It is not completely unregulated. Federal candidates have a $5,000 **hard money** limit on the amount they may receive from the PACs, $1,000 from individuals. The U.S. Federal Elections Commission closely monitors campaign fund-raising reports. Rules for other elections

The anti-abortion group Right to Life, like other private issue activists, provides strong financial support to political campaigns.

vary from state to state. Smart politicians study the rules carefully and know them inside and out.

Individual donors are a crucial source of political money. During the 1992 presidential campaign, Democratic candidate Jerry Brown enlisted thousands of individual donors, limited to $100 each. By the end of the campaign, when the other candidates were broke, Brown's $100 donations kept rolling in, keeping him in the race long after Clinton had sewn up the nomination.

Many attempts to reform campaign finance have been made, especially since the Watergate scandal of 1974. The best-known attempt is the McCain-Feingold bill, which would curb the practice of giving so-called **soft money** to the major parties.

Soft money refers to the huge corporate contributions political parties are allowed to receive. This is in excess of the $5,000 PAC limits federal candidates must observe. The practice of funneling soft money through the parties lets big donors skirt federal limits on gifts to candidates.

Campaign finance reforms have been largely unsuccessful because the U.S. Supreme Court consistently rules against them as an infringement of free speech. Many legal scholars now support a constitutional amendment that would clearly separate free speech from campaign money.

One politician who has fought every recent reform effort is U.S. Senator Mitch McConnell (Republican from Kentucky). Senator McConnell is an enthusiastic supporter of political money, both hard and soft. He believes that PACs and corporations should be allowed to use their money as they see fit. "Be it bumper stickers on your car, yard signs on your lawn or the voluntary contribution of your hard-earned money to the candidates or party of your choosing—these are all constitutionally protected means of participation in our democracy," McConnell has said.

Candidates for public office are faced with difficult choices: How do you obtain the money you need to run

Vice President Al Gore mingles with the audience at a fund-raiser for his 2000 presidential campaign. The financial support of individual donors like these can be crucial.

for office without being compromised? How do you reconcile your need for money and preserve your integrity at the same time? It is not easy, but it can be done. There are officials in both major parties who manage it with relative degrees of success. The main problem in accepting any contribution is the sense of obligation it creates in the recipient.

Human nature requires the paying back of favors, especially financial ones. A cash gift to a candidate means a return favor down the line. It may be the courtesy of a friendly greeting, a phone call, or a good word. But the giver invariably wants some future payback from the gift.

Most observers believe that in the present climate, anybody who wants to become an elected official must play the game. In fact, following the money is considered a mark of professionalism by the power brokers. Beginning candidates need to do some soul-searching and decide where they will obtain contributions.

Raising money will be a constant chore for anyone feeling the tug of political ambition. You will have to work at it, but be on guard. The power brokers who have political money are always well-dressed and well-spoken. They appear genuinely interested in seeing you get ahead in your political career. Occasionally their interest is sincere. They would never intentionally cause harm or problems an opponent might use against you.

There are some, even among those who run the PACs, who feel uncomfortable with the present system. They fear it is corrupt and dislike the politician's endless demands for money. Whatever the future of our political finance system, those who dislike it are far more numerous than those who favor it.

Some politicians continually pester the political action committees for money. A few well-financed candidates are failures at the ballot box. Senator Rudy Boschwitz, a Republican from Minnesota, loved collecting money from virtually any source. When Boschwitz lost in 1990, he out-spent the candidate who beat him by a 5-to-1 margin. Sometimes money isn't everything.

However, in most cases, in order to run an effective campaign, you will need an enormous amount of money. To get the money to run your campaign, you may have to solicit funds from the corporate PACs. There are some candidates who refuse to do this and will accept money only from individuals and then only in small amounts. With a couple of notable exceptions, most of the PAC-free candidates have been known to lose elections.

Probably the most common approach to political fund raising is one of grudging acceptance. You don't really want to ask PACs and rich people for money, but there is no way around it if you want to get elected. And you can't do anything unless you win. So you pick up the phone and make the necessary calls.

At any rate, the successful accumulation of money allows a candidate to plan his or her campaign. On that score, some PACs are better than others. For example, a special PAC exists that supports female candidates. It is called EMILY's List. The word EMILY stands for "Early Money Is Like Yeast." The reference suggests that early money keeps on rising.

As money comes in, it also goes out, typically being spent on phones, mailings, signs, literature, radio, and occasionally television, when enough is available for it.

If the race heats up, the need for money grows. The level of campaign activity is about equal to the amount of money available to spend on it. How the money raised from PACs and individuals gets spent is the essence of any campaign.

Former British Prime Minister Winston Churchill (second from right), shown campaigning in England in 1950, believed that getting elected was the best training for successfully holding office.

CHAPTER 4

Campaigning to Win

SOME POLITICIANS CONSIDER RUNNING for office a great thrill. For others, it is a trying chore. Whether you love it or hate it, the goal for any serious candidate is victory. During hard fought election campaigns, candidates bring every available resource to bear on the task of winning.

Former British Prime Minister Winston Churchill said the fighting and winning of election campaigns was the best education for successfully holding office. From the highest to the lowest, successful political candidates must return to the people again and again for support. Nothing can be taken for granted and much learning takes place during the campaign process.

The competition can be extremely intense. Politics in America is like a bare-knuckle prizefight. Unknown to many people, the stakes are extremely high. The federal government alone spends trillions of dollars annually. In 1998, elections of all kinds consumed $2 billion.

The offices ranged from local animal control officers to senators of the United States. People don't spend that kind of money without good reason.

Conducting a Successful Campaign

There are many ways to conduct a successful campaign. One highly recommended method is to plan your campaign carefully. Campaign manuals of many kinds are available at the library. You should check them out and see if any of the tips apply to your campaign. Read what other people say about running for office and give the idea some serious thought. Talk to friends, family, and power brokers. Don't rush off in a burst of enthusiasm.

Be sure to comply with the basic requirements for the office you plan to seek. Are you registered in the political party that has the nomination you want? Are you old enough to run? Do you live in the district? Will a person of your outlook have a chance of winning there? If not, perhaps you should move elsewhere or seek a different office. These may seem like simple questions, but many promising candidacies have been undone by them.

Once you are satisfied that you are eligible to run, the next order of business is to call a meeting with your closest supporters. Map out a plan. It should describe in detail how you expect to win. Put your plan down on paper and check it from time to time. Make changes if necessary. You may want to allow some flexibility but try to follow your campaign plan as much as possible.

First and foremost is the issue of money. When Paul Laxalt decided to run for governor of Nevada, the first thing he did was appoint a treasurer to oversee fundraising. The importance of having enough money to run your campaign cannot be overstated. It is critical to remember that people must be asked to contribute. Fundraisers must raise funds. If one treasurer can't deliver, you should appoint another. As a candidate, you will be expected to do much of the money asking. Don't be shy. Even at high-ranking campaigns like the presidency, candidates still have to make a certain quota of calls to solicit money.

For a politician with ambition, every waking moment is a quest for votes. The campaign never really stops. During a formal campaign, however, the level of activity is stepped up. Sometimes it can be unbelievably frantic.

Who Votes

A typical election campaign begins the instant you decide you are going to run and ends the moment the last vote is cast. Right up to election night, candidates will do everything in their power to influence the decision. They

Voters line up to cast their ballots in a presidential election. About a third of registered voters remain undecided up to election day.

must hustle to the last minute because many voters don't make up their minds until the night before or even the day of the election. These undecided voters are a major political battleground. Candidates go to great lengths to capture the undecided vote.

Strangely enough, political scientists have learned that undecided voters are typically the most ill-informed and least politically active of our citizens. On average they number about one-third of the registered voters. It is ironic but true that the undecided voters eventually determine who most of our elected officials will be.

People who strongly believe in one political party over another are called hard-core party identifiers. They usually have their minds made up long before an election takes place. The party identifiers nearly always vote for the candidates of their own party. They do this, it is believed, because they grew up in families where politics was taken seriously. During childhood their parents supported a political party or discussed in depth the issues of the day. They grew up believing politics is important.

Not every family is like that. A lot of people grow up believing that politics is an unwelcome bother. They do not care who is president or what policies we follow. If they vote at all, they do it with a low-level of enthusiasm. A large number of people (about half the population) rarely or never vote.

Although elections convey tremendous power on the winner, it is sometimes hard to get people to pay attention. You would think it would be different. As one of the world's oldest democracies, Americans have come to expect the orderly exchange of power. Even our military forces respect the civilian government. A president with no military background can give orders to the armed forces and be confident those orders will be carried out. Thankfully, no American president has ever been forced from office by military action. Despite low participation, Americans are blessed in their political traditions.

Because the stakes are so high, political campaigning is a serious business. The toughest and brightest candidates find ways to win. The occasional refusal of support must be overlooked in the ongoing search for votes. If one person says no, there are many others who will say yes. The job of the candidate and the campaign is to find potential supporters and get them to the polls.

Surprisingly, many nonvoters have strong opinions if you ask them direct questions. Candidates frequently come across such people while making their rounds. The nonvoters complain about some governmental practice. They express outrage over school costs or oppose big business, labor unions, or high taxes.

Candidates listen politely and note their concerns. Before they leave, they check the **precinct** walking list. No name is listed because the person has never registered to vote.

Just above the nonvoters on the political scale are the rare voters. When it comes to voting, rare voters normally fall in the undecided category. For these folks, politics is like a low-interest spectator sport. They would like to see their team win but are not going to cry if it doesn't. This is not the case in many other countries, where the outcome of an election means life or death for thousands of party or candidate supporters.

In a two-candidate race, as most partisan general election battles are, even a poor campaign will nearly always capture one-third of the voters, perhaps more. At the very least, you can expect your hard-core party identifiers to support you. At either end of the spectrum, the party identifiers cancel each other out. That leaves the undecideds.

In a really top-notch campaign, you will win your party supporters and most of the undecideds. Such a victory is called a landslide. More often, the undecideds will split, with the victory going to the candidate who wins the larger portion of them.

Street Campaigning

"Winning the streets," or street campaigning, is a sure-fire way to win a political campaign. To help win the streets, a candidate will need many volunteers. Sources of volunteers are among the people whose causes you support. Other places to look are at colleges, high schools, labor unions, and civic groups of all kinds. Asking the people you meet while campaigning is the best source of all.

Volunteers are a critical part of any campaign organization. Recruiting people to work on your campaign requires asking them to lend you a hand. Chances are they won't help unless they are asked. Part of your campaign duties are to keep on asking.

Labor-intensive work, like distributing leaflets, is made easy by having many hands available to help out. The best time of the week to start handing out information is the late morning on a Saturday, close to 10:00 A.M. Volunteers can get in a good three hours work before breaking for a late lunch. A group of the candidate's family, friends, and supporters meet at a prearranged place to begin leafleting. Areas are marked out and people are supplied with literature, precinct walking lists, and street maps. The best lists are arranged so that your volunteers won't have to waste time trying to figure out where they are.

In most cases volunteers will travel in pairs for safety and practical considerations. Walking an election precinct is an education no one should miss. Voters are sorted by age, address, gender, and party affiliation on county registration lists.

You can tell a lot about people by knowing where they live, their gender, their age, and their party affiliation. After a while people seem pretty much the same to politicians. It doesn't take long before you begin to recognize types and understand what they desire in a leader.

No one in a campaign should be above the gritty work of street campaigning. A candidate who refuses to go out among the people to seek support will most likely lose. A candidate who is unafraid of going out among the people will eventually be a winner.

Effectively using a candidate's time is something all campaigns strive to do. A potentially successful campaign will divide major organizational chores, with an eye toward making the best use of available time resources.

Appointing one person as treasurer of the campaign is considered a good division of labor. If possible, someone else should serve as campaign coordinator. These people ought to be close to the candidate, having his or her confidence and trust. They should also be assertive, unafraid to pick up the phone and ask for help, ask for a donation, or complain to the media about poor coverage.

The Media

The media does not normally play an important part in campaigns below the city, state, or congressional level. Other than the occasional newspaper endorsement, local elections go largely unreported. A common misconception people have about the media, particularly newspaper and television reporters, is that they are somehow more knowledgeable. This is often not the case.

Most of the time, media people know as little about what is going on in political circles as ordinary citizens do—that is, almost nothing. Some media people can be shockingly ignorant about the varied responsibilities of elected officials. Some may even pay more attention to sports heroes and movie stars than they do to elections. It is a special circumstance when the media reports on a local candidate.

In low-visibility races, mailings are an expensive but effective tool for getting your message to the voters. Printed materials should be well-written, easy to understand, and free from errors. Flashing an attractive brochure that puts your best foot forward has a strong appeal. Candidates often include photos of their families to show they are connected to ordinary concerns.

Reform Party candidate Ross Perot (right) appears in a televised interview on Larry King Live. *Television exposure is essential in a national election.*

Only in rare cases will television advertising be used in a race smaller than a congressional district election. When local candidates go on television, something significant could be about to happen.

People spend enormous amounts of their leisure time watching television. On average, adults spend four hours per day watching television. Having a sharp television ad can put an unknown candidate "on the map" and help build name familiarity. In big races, TV is critical. National and statewide television political spots are guaranteed to reach large audiences.

A candidate will spend a lot of time attending political meetings of various sorts. Political party meetings soak up the time of partisan candidates. There are also neighborhood meetings, candidate's fairs, visits with lobbyists, meetings with power brokers, and election fund-raisers.

All functions will eat heavily into a busy candidate's time. Appearances at lengthy meetings therefore must be rationed out. They take up a lot of time and few voters attend them. Veteran candidates usually put in a quick appearance and then move on as soon as possible.

Meanwhile, you keep plugging away, trying to get people interested in your campaign. National figures show that not quite half of eligible Americans are registered to vote. As income and education goes up, so does participation in the political system. It is too bad that those who stand to gain the most from political activity, like the young, minorities, and the poor, participate the least in our system. Dramatic shifts might occur if more people ran for office and voted as often as do seniors and the wealthy.

Low participation in the system is a worry, but things are looking better. The National Commission on Civic Renewal, chaired by former Georgia Senator Sam Nunn, issued a June 1999 report that said more Americans are becoming politically involved. It is heartening news for people concerned about the process.

Americans who attended a political rally or speech rose from 5.5 percent of adults to 6.5 percent between 1994 and 1997. The number who worked for a political party rose from 2.7 percent to 3.4 percent. On the downside, however, the number who voted fell from 47 percent in 1994 to 43 percent in 1997.

Despite the improvement in some figures, less than half of the adult population makes all the political decisions for the rest of us. Candidates tailor their messages for this small but politically active group.

Richard Nixon (right) was presidential candidate Dwight D. Eisenhower's (left) running mate in the 1956 election. Nixon later earned the nickname "Tricky Dick" for his sometimes questionable methods of fighting back against his opponents.

CHAPTER 5

Fighting Back Effectively

On the Attack

FORMER PRESIDENT RICHARD NIXON had a reputation as a rough, dirty campaigner. Nixon's original instructor in this regard was a California political consultant named Murray Chotiner.

Chotiner's motto was to always be on the attack in a campaign. By that he meant you should bring up—again and again—anything that made you look good and your opponent look bad. Nixon followed Chotiner's cynical advice all the way to the White House. The Nixon presidency lasted from 1969 until 1974, when illegal activities came to light. The ensuing Watergate scandal forced Nixon to become the only president who has ever resigned.

The political scene is crowded with aggressive candidates. A successful candidate must therefore learn how to cope with an attack. Not every day on the campaign trail will be a good one. Things won't always go right. There will be times when you blurt out the wrong thing or wind up defending yourself in front of a hostile audience. Anything can happen.

Techniques for Overcoming Adversity

Joint appearances with other candidates are a common type of campaign event. At them you will learn to participate in a lot of give-and-take with others in a public forum. Once in a while the media will be there to report the proceedings. You must learn to think on your feet and have solid answers for tough questions. Otherwise your opponent may distort the things you say and people will believe him or her.

No matter what your background or personality, the best approach is to keep things in perspective. You must maintain your balance in good times and bad. A poor day is not the end of the world. There are clever ways to fight back. Despite varying personal styles, most successful candidates recommend a handful of reliable techniques to overcome adversity:

1. Don't panic.
2. Use humor to your advantage.
3. Know about the problems of ordinary people.
4. Admit your mistakes.
5. Be courageous.

1. Don't Panic.

If you are serious about seeking office, it is important to be ready to bounce back at all times. Once you are in the race, emotions will often dominate. Everything that goes well for you will generate wild optimism. When things go wrong there is a tendency to panic.

Remember, most people are only paying slight attention to you. A large majority of people find politics tiresome and dull, although they will not usually admit it.

Deep down, they know it is probably important but they just can't bring themselves to pay much attention to it.

So don't get too upset when you make a mistake. Don't stay focused on what you did wrong. Instead think about what you need to do to repair the damage and put the best possible face on your efforts to make it right. Chances are people will forget your mistake and remember your repair efforts afterwards.

2. Use Humor to Your Advantage.

Opposing politicians will probably have no trouble finding out everything negative they need to know about you. Your every goof will be gift wrapped and delivered to their door. They will learn about every traffic ticket, school failure, and reprimand you have ever received.

Nothing disarms critics like a sense of humor. It often works to make a joke in an uncomfortable situation. During his career in Parliament, Winston Churchill used humor to defend himself when a fellow member attacked him for changing political parties.

Churchill got cheers and laughter by replying: "I said a lot of stupid things when I worked with the Conservative Party, and I left it because I did not want to go on saying stupid things."

As a senator from New York, Robert Kennedy was not noted for his interest in agricultural issues. While Kennedy was speaking outdoors in a brisk wind one day, a tiny piece of paper blew off the podium. It fluttered into the crowd. "Hey, get that back for me," Kennedy said. "That's my farm policy."

Former Kansas Senator Bob Dole has long been admired for his quick-witted asides. During his 1996 presidential campaign, Dole was asked to identify the most important quality voters would want to know about him. Dole replied: "Beats me."

Dole was also humorous in his treatment of other political figures, including high officeholders. No one who heard it will forget Dole's description of former Presidents Ford, Carter, and Nixon as "See No Evil, Hear No Evil, and Evil."

Perhaps Dole's most famous joke came at the expense of Nixon as well. When it was revealed that Nixon had secretly taped every Oval Office conversation, Dole said: "Thank God I only nodded when I was in there."

During the presidential campaign of 1972, seemingly minor charges against the candidates suddenly began to fly right and left. The rank atmosphere cleared only after Senator George McGovern came forward to make a confession.

The senator told the press that he had stolen a watermelon from a neighbor's field when he was a boy. McGovern said he was sorry about the watermelon and promised to make amends.

Senator George McGovern made skillful use of humor in the 1972 presidential campaign to embarrass reporters about the irrelevance of some of their charges.

The press laughed an embarrassed laughter. Though they had been reporting charges against the candidates almost daily, they now began to back off. Using just a touch of his patented deadpan humor, McGovern had whistled foul on the petty campaign charges. The reporters soon turned to more relevant issues.

3. Know About the Problems of Ordinary People.

Knowing about the problems of ordinary people can help you avoid an embarrassing mistake. A good example is the northwest congressman who was asked to price some common household items. It happened as he was running for an open seat in the U.S. Senate. The question was a trick to find out how much he knew about the problems ordinary people must face. Among the items listed were the price of a pair of blue jeans, a loaf of bread, and a gallon of milk. Because he rarely shopped at stores, the congressman did not know what the items cost. His performance in front of the television cameras was a complete disaster. Even worse, his opponent chimed in with all the correct answers, one after the other, right down the line.

Instead of falling apart, the congressman admitted he didn't have the answers but was going to learn them. The next time out, he was much better prepared. However, in his initial answers, the congressman revealed that he was indeed far removed from the problems of ordinary people. His ignorance of common concerns showed through, nearly costing him the election.

4. Admit Your Mistakes.

Candidates should be aware of the things that might be used against them and prepare a defense in advance.

Let's assume that you have decided you will no longer accept money from political action committees. Unfortunately, you have made a practice of taking the money in the past. But from now on you are determined to refuse contributions that might compromise your integrity. You announce that you won't accept any more PAC money and play it up heavily in your election campaign.

You also start criticizing your opponent, who still takes money from the PACs. You claim your opponent is bought and paid for, the same thing you hear from people as you go door-to-door. The charges sting your opponent, as always happens when someone speaks the truth.

Soon you are scheduled to meet your opponent in a joint appearance. What do you think your opponent will do? He or she will be ready to pounce on your past acceptance of PAC money. Your opponent will try to use it against you, to prove that you are a hypocrite.

In this situation, your strategy should be to beat your opponent to the punch. Honestly admit that you took PAC money in the past but now consider it a mistake. You have made a pledge never to do it again. If your opponent keeps saying that you are being hypocritical, it will remind everyone that he or she still takes the PAC money. Your chances of winning are still good.

Although they may not know much about who is running for office at any given time, ordinary citizens know what is right and what is wrong. They can be very forgiving of human mistakes, as long as they don't involve lying, cheating, or stealing. It is all right to change your mind or say you were wrong. You might add, incidentally, that you plan to do better in the future.

5. Be Courageous.

No successful politician will ignore the basic truths about human nature. One truth is that hardly anyone will support a cause without expecting some clear benefit from it.

Another truth is that people are more emotional than they are rational. In other words, you get further with appeals to their emotions than you do by appealing to their intelligence or common sense. What you do with your

knowledge of human nature will define you as a politician. It will also be critical to your success when you become an elected official. The best politicians develop a tender attitude toward people, despite their faults. Lincoln called this tenderness "malice toward none."

It takes a great deal of courage to love and respect people when you know as much about them as any politician does. You want to avoid becoming the kind of tired, cynical former officeholder who says nothing ever changes. Insights that politicians glean in the course of their careers are often painful. Seeking elective office is a hard, punishing profession that constantly hammers away at your outlook on life. Only the strongest and best rise above it.

Maybe you could be one of them.

Because most people cannot easily forgive a politician for lying, President Clinton had to apologize numerous times for misleading the public about his affair with White House intern Monica Lewinsky.

CHAPTER **6**

Making a Difference

AFTER ALL THE HUSTLING, fund-raising, public meetings, street campaigning, speeches, and voting, you find yourself taking the oath of office. It is only now that the reality of what you have done finally begins to sink in. You are an elected official. It is time to do your job. But you must also look to the next election, the next campaign. If not for yourself, then for your party or your supporters.

The campaign manuals provided you with good tips on how to get yourself elected. They told you what to say and what to do in a variety of situations. The process of vote getting is a fairly straightforward business, with clear rules and procedures. Yet there is much more to becoming an elected official than simply collecting more votes than your opponent.

Prepare yourself for many long hours of sitting in a chair, politely listening to people explain things. More hours will be spent with people in social settings. Everybody wants to persuade you to see things his or her way. The listening goes on and on, day after day. No doubt you want to do something important with your new power. You want to make a difference. It is easier said than done. Once they take office, politicians soon discover that they do not have unlimited freedom of action. They come face-to-face with pressures to produce results acceptable to all factions.

Elected officials try to achieve what is called **consensus** as much as possible. That means forging a decision everybody can live with, whether they like it or not. More than anything else, politicians have the responsibility of refereeing the conflicts that arise between competing groups in our society. The incessant fighting can be very aggravating. After you have heard it all and discussed it many times, you cast your vote. Sometimes it doesn't matter how you vote, as long as the other players know why you did it and can accept your explanation.

Make no mistake: in the United States, serving in elected office means protecting the people who have money. For the most part, the people with money are directors and stockholders of corporations, especially large corporations. These people have power to make and break elected officials. You cannot cross them very often without facing their determined opposition come election time.

Given the opportunity, they will be happy to put an end to your political career, leaving you in the wistful role of "has been." To remain in office, you must always recognize the power of wealthy interests and act accordingly.

On the other hand, there are people with no money and no influence with elected officials. Such people include the sick, the disabled, unskilled workers, immigrants, the very young, the poor, and most ordinary citizens. The majority of people are so consumed by their own problems they have little time to spend on governmental debates, issues, initiatives, and legislation.

Be smart. If you are going climb the elected official ladder, you will have to stake out your turf. Ambitious young politicians find it to their advantage to specialize. They learn they must become an expert on some subject that will require others to defer to them. Before coming to Washington, Lyndon Johnson had been a poor boy. All he really had was his remarkable political talent and a degree from Southwest State Teacher's College in San Marcos, Texas. By the time he was elected Senate Majority Leader in the 1950s, Johnson was so completely an expert on the ways of the Congress that he literally ran the show.

Although he rose to the highest office in the land when he became president, Johnson never forgot his roots. He remembered what it had been like to be a nobody, a person without important connections. Johnson loved politics because he felt it was a job where talent counted. In the Senate Johnson knew how to mark up a bill, sweet talk an opponent, sell an idea, and **bamboozle** a lobbyist like no one else. If you wanted to get a bill through Congress, you had to deal with Johnson, sooner or later.

President Lyndon B. Johnson discusses civil rights objectives with Roy Wilkins, executive secretary of the NAACP, in 1963. Johnson gained great political power by becoming an expert on the way to get things done in Congress.

At the same time Johnson paid close attention to the folks back home in Texas. A large part of every officeholder's job is **constituent** casework.

People often run into problems with government agencies and look to politicians to assist them whenever possible. Not every favor seeker is a corporation looking to improve its bottom line. Many times elected officials must explain what agencies are doing and why they are doing it. People depend on elected officials to intervene when something goes wrong. This intervention is an important safety valve for citizens.

The elderly woman who has been denied government benefits or the disabled child in need of special placement are examples of the kinds of people elected officials assist. Staff members are hired, themselves often former government workers, to do vast amounts of constituent casework. The elected officials who hire the best constituent staff are more likely to remain in office. Those who ignore their constituents will find themselves voted out in short order.

Johnson got ahead by learning all about Congress from friends like House Speaker Sam Rayburn and Georgia Senator Richard Russell. An elected official today will find it wise to become an expert on taxation, capital improvement law, human resource issues, education, social services, criminal justice, or any one of the many areas that come up regularly for legislative review. Building power in your job by developing expertise in a particular field is a smart way to stay ahead of the game.

Sometimes it takes years to gather the knowledge necessary to develop that special expertise. The advent of **term limits** in the 21st century means that there is less opportunity than ever to get a handle on your job. A byproduct of term limits on officeholders is that you will have only a short period of time in which to make your mark. Voters have imposed term limits on some elective offices because a feeling exists that too many officeholders treat their jobs as lifetime appointments.

Representative Floyd Prozanski is an Oregon State legislator facing the end of his House service as a result of term limits. He spoke philosophically about his six years as an elected official:

"My time in the legislature has been somewhat of a mixed bag," Prozanski said. "Being in the minority party, I haven't been able to work on pro-active legislation to the level that I wanted. On the other hand, I have been able to provide a defense, keeping some poor, bad public policy from taking effect, with the assistance of the governor being willing and able to veto bad bills."

Right away, newly elected officials find out many unpleasant facts about government in general. The inside world of politics is not a bed of roses. The people in it are tough and ruthless. The recent political history of the United States is, fortunately, not as blood-stained as that of many other nations. Still, there are ever-present dangers in seeking office.

In the last 50 years, one president (John F. Kennedy) has been assassinated and another, Ronald Reagan, has been shot. An unsuccessful attempt was made on the life of President Gerald Ford in 1975.

Senator Robert Kennedy was killed while campaigning for president in 1968. Four years later another presidential hopeful, Alabama Governor George Wallace, was shot several times at close range and as a result was paralyzed for life. Except for President Kennedy's murderer, all the shooters remain in prison to this day.

Lesser politicians are by no means safe either. In San Francisco, Mayor George Moscone and Supervisor Harvey Milk were each killed by one of their colleagues.

People would not try to kill our leaders if they were not doing something important. Despite the many unpleasant choices and compromises our political leaders must make, giving your energy, your spirit, and possibly your life to public service is truly a high calling. In no other vocation can you find out more about what really makes people tick.

Alabama Governor George C. Wallace (in wheelchair) was shot and paralyzed while campaigning for the presidency in 1972. Assassination attempts are one of the dangers of seeking office.

You learn the secrets of leadership by seeking to become a leader. If you fail, there is nothing dishonorable about it. If you succeed, you can change the world for generations to come.

In the United States elected officials have made the most critical decisions any human being can make. Abraham Lincoln, on his own authority as commander in chief, freed millions of slaves during the Civil War. Another elected official, President Harry Truman, ordered the use of nuclear weapons to shorten World War II, thus saving millions of American lives.

There is more than one way to change things. **Jim Crow** laws were successfully attacked with widespread

civil disobedience in the 1950s and 1960s. However, it was the Congress of the United States that made the end of Jim Crow official with the passage of the Civil Rights Act of 1964. No longer could the states discriminate against African-American citizens. Perhaps our elected officials aren't the best ones to break the glass of injustice, but they can do a pretty good clean-up job afterwards.

For all the time and trouble it takes, competing for the leadership of your community, state, or nation is a rewarding pursuit. Victory will be obtained only after strenuous effort. Long hours are spent with people wanting you to see things their way. If you seek elective office at all, you will do it because you know how important it is. The job of being a leader is never completely finished. The political process, like life, is forever in a state of evolution.

Decisions that elected officials make ripple on down through the years, both good and bad. In the end, if you keep the faith, believing in the fruits of democracy, you might make the world a better place in which to live.

President Harry S. Truman holds up the famous erroneous headline announcing his defeat in 1948. Three years earlier, Truman had made the decision to hasten the end of World War II by dropping an atomic bomb on Hiroshima, Japan.

Glossary

Advertising—In political campaigns, the signs, buttons, brochures, and other commercial materials produced to help a candidate win an election.

Bamboozle—Pulling one over on somebody; in politics it means deceiving by underhanded methods.

Campaign—The personal efforts of a candidate, supporters, and financial backers to win an elective office.

Consensus—Getting people to agree on a single course of action, even though they might not like it.

Constituent—A citizen residing in the electoral district of a legislator or other elected official.

Corporation—A group of people chartered to operate a business, usually for profit.

Filing—The formal start of a political race.

General election—An election pitting partisan candidates against each other, usually held in November of even-numbered years.

Hard money—The $1,000 amounts individuals may give to federal candidates and the $5,000 amounts PACs may give to federal candidates.

Hegemony—Having a dominant influence over others in the political realm.

Jim Crow—Laws meant to separate white and black Americans from each other in public accommodations. In practice, Jim Crow gave blacks an inferior status.

Political action committee—A group of people who organize to influence elections by collecting money to spend on them.

Precinct—A small portion of an electoral district from which voting results are reported.

Primary election—An election used to nominate party candidates, who then face the candidates of other political parties in a general election.

Glossary

Soft money—Big contributions that go through political parties in excess of the limits federal candidates must observe.

Term limits—Preventing, by law, a candidate from seeking more than a set number of terms in office.

Further Reading

Feinberg, Barbara Silberdick. *Term Limits for Congress?* Brookfield, CT: Twenty-First Century Books, 1996.

Health, David. *Elections in the United States.* Mankato, MN: Capstone Publishing, 1999.

Jones, Veda Boyd. *Government & Politics.* Philadelphia: Chelsea House, 1999.

O'Leary, Bradley S., and Kamber, Victor. *Are You a Republican or a Democrat?* Lanham, MD: Boru Publishing, 1998.

Sandak, Cass R. *Lobbying: Inside Government.* Brookfield, CT: Twenty-First Century Books, 1996.

Sullivan, George. *Campaigns and Elections: Ballots and Bandwagons.* Upper Saddle River, NJ: Silver Burdett Press, 1991.

Witcover, Jules. *The Resurrection of Richard Nixon.* New York: Putnam, 1970.

Index

Baschwitz, Rudy, 32–33
Bill, 55, 57
Brown, Jerry, 30

Campaigning, 9
    door-to-door, 21–23
    and the media, 41–44
    street, 40–41
Camus, Albert, 15
Candidate
    recruited, 11–13
    self-starter, 13–14
Carter, Jimmy, 48
Chotiner, Murray, 45
Churchill, Winston, 35, 47
Civil Rights Act, 59
Civil War, 18, 58
Clinton, Bill, 30
Clinton, Hillary, 18
Common Cause, 25
Congress, 9, 10, 55, 59

Dole, Bob, 27, 47–48
Douglas, Stephen, 13

Elected officials
    and deciding to run, 9–15
    responsibilities of, 53–60
    and successful campaign-
        ing, 36–37
    types of candidates, 11–14
EMILY, 33

Federal Elections Commission,
    27

Ford, Gerald, 48, 57

General election, 18

Hard money, 29–33
House of Representatives, 10,
    25

Interest groups, 21

Jim Crow, 58–59
Johnson, Lyndon B., 55

Kennedy, John F., 57
Kennedy, Robert F., 15, 47, 57

Lincoln, Abraham, 13, 17, 51,
    58

McCain-Feingold Bill, 30
McConnell, Mitch, 31
McGovern, George, 48
Milk, Harvey, 57
Moscone, George, 57

Nader, Ralph, 28
National Commission of Civic
    Renewal, 43
Nixon, Richard, 10, 45, 48

Nunn, Sam, 43

Partisan races, 12
Political action committees
    (PACs), 27, 29–33, 58
Political parties, 12, 30, 36, 38,
    42, 43
Power brokers, 19–21, 42
Primary election, 18
Private issue groups, 29
Prozanski, Floyd, 14, 57

Rayburn, Sam, 56
Rogers, Will, 25
Russell, Richard, 56

Senate, 18, 25
Soft money, 29–33
Supreme Court, 27, 31

Truman, Harry, 58

Wallace, George, 57
World War II, 58

ABOUT THE AUTHOR: Mike Bonner is the author of many books for school children. In 1986 Bonner was elected to the Metropolitan Service District Council, the regional government covering the Portland, Oregon area. Bonner also spent two sessions serving as a legislative assistant in the Oregon House of Representatives. He has worked on many political campaigns, beginning as a student volunteer for legendary Oregon Senator Wayne Morse. In 1993, Bonner was elected county chair of his political party, serving until 1995.

A graduate of the University of Oregon, with a degree in political science, Bonner currently resides in Eugene, Oregon. He is married to Carol Kleinheksel. Mike and Carol have a daughter, Karen, who attends public middle school.

SENIOR CONSULTING EDITOR Arthur M. Schlesinger, jr. is the leading American historian of our time. He won the Pulitzer Prize for his book *The Age of Jackson* (1945) and again for *A Thousand Days* (1965). This chronicle of the Kennedy Administration also won a National Book Award. Professor Schlesinger is the Albert Schweitzer Professor of the Humanities at the City University of New York, and has been involved in several other Chelsea House projects, including the REVOLUTIONARY WAR LEADERS and COLONIAL LEADERS series.